THE
STRONG-WILLED CHILD
BIBLE STUDY

SURVIVING BIRTH THROUGH ADOLESCENCE

DR. JAMES DOBSON

developed with Michael O'Neal

LifeWay Press®
Nashville, Tennessee

Published by LifeWay Press®
© 2014 Siggie, LLC
Reprinted 2014

The New Strong-Willed Child © 2014 by Dr. James Dobson. Published by Tyndale House Publishers; Carol Stream, IL. Used by Permission.

ISBN: 978-1-4300-3299-1
Item: 005650400

Dewey decimal classification: 649
Subject headings: CHILD REARING \ CHILD PSYCHOLOGY \ CHILD DEVELOPMENT

Unless indicated otherwise, all Scripture quotations are taken from the Holman Christian Standard Bible. Copyright © 1999, 2000, 2002, 2003, 2009 by Holman Bible Publishers. Used by permission. Holman Christian Standard Bible® and HCSB® are federally registered trademarks of Holman Bible Publishers. All Scripture quotations marked (NIV) are taken from Holy Bible, NEW INTERNATIONAL VERSION®. Copyright © 1973, 1978, 1984 by Biblica, Inc. All rights reserved worldwide. Used by permission.

Cover photo: Ron Chapple Studios/Thinkstock.

To order additional copies of this resource, write to LifeWay Church Resources, Customer Service, One LifeWay Plaza, Nashville, TN 37234-0113; fax 615.251.5933; phone 800.458.2772; order online at *www.lifeway.com* or email *orderentry@lifeway.com*; or visit the LifeWay Christian Store serving you.

Printed in the United States of America

Adult Ministry Publishing, LifeWay Church Resources, One LifeWay Plaza, Nashville, TN 37234-0152

Contents

About the Author. 4

How to Use This Study. 5

Guidelines for Groups 6

Introduction. 7

WEEK 1
Childish or Defiant Behavior?. 9

WEEK 2
Who's in Charge?. 21

WEEK 3
Good News for All 33

WEEK 4
Let Love Be Your Guide 45

Key Insights. 57

Leader Notes 58

Further Resources 60

Introducing Your Child To Christ. 61

About the Author

DR. JAMES DOBSON is the founder and president of Family Talk, a nonprofit organization that produces his radio program, "Dr. James Dobson's Family Talk." He is the author of more than 50 books dedicated to the preservation of the family, including *The New Dare to Discipline*; *Love for a Lifetime*; *Life on the Edge*; *Love Must Be Tough*; *The New Strong-Willed Child*; *When God Doesn't Make Sense*; *Bringing Up Boys*; *Bringing Up Girls*; *Head Over Heels*; and, most recently, *Dr. Dobson's Handbook of Family Advice*.

Dr. Dobson served as an associate clinical professor of pediatrics at the University of Southern California School of Medicine for fourteen years and on the attending staff of Children's Hospital of Los Angeles for seventeen years in the divisions of Child Development and Medical Genetics. He has been active in governmental affairs and has advised three United States presidents on family matters.

In 1967 he earned his PhD in child development from the University of Southern California and holds eighteen honorary doctoral degrees. In 2009 he was inducted into the National Radio Hall of Fame.

Dr. Dobson and his wife, Shirley, reside in Colorado Springs, Colorado. They have two grown children, Danae and Ryan, and two grandchildren.

MICHAEL O'NEAL is minister of education and missions at First Baptist Church, Cumming, Georgia. He has also served as youth minister, worship leader, associate pastor, church planter, and college/seminary professor. He and his wife, Carrie, are parents to two boys.

How to Use This Study

The four sessions of this study may be used weekly or during a weekend retreat. But we recommend that before you dig into this material, you watch the film *The Strong-Willed Child* from the *Dr. James Dobson Presents: Building a Family Legacy* film series. This will lay the groundwork for your study.

This material has been written for a small-group experience, for you and your spouse, or for personal study.

An option to extend or conclude this study is for your group to view the film *Your Legacy* from the *Dr. James Dobson Presents: Building a Family Legacy* film series.

CONNECT: The purpose of the introductory section of each session invites and motivates you to connect with the topic of the session and others in your group.

WATCH: The study DVD contains four DVD clips which include introductions from Ryan Dobson and clips from a talk by Dr. James Dobson, based on the film and the accompanying book *The New Strong-Willed Child* by Dr. Dobson (Tyndale Momentum; ISBN 978-1-4143-9134-2.)

ENGAGE: This section is the primary focus of each week's group time. You and other participants will further engage the truths of Scripture and discuss accompanying questions. This section will also include a Wrap Up portion, which concludes the group session and leads to the Reflect section.

REFLECT: This at-home study section helps you dig deeper into Scripture and apply the truths you're learning. Go deeper each week by reading the suggested chapters in the book *The New Strong-Willed Child* and completing the activities at the end of each session in this study.

Guidelines for Groups

While you can complete this study alone, you will benefit greatly from covering the material with your spouse or with the interaction of a Sunday School class or small group. Here are a few ways to cultivate a valuable experience as you engage in this study.

PREPARATION: To get the most out of each group time, read through the study each week and answer the questions so you're ready to discuss the material. It will also be helpful for you and your group members to have copies of the book *The New Strong-Willed Child* (ISBN 978-1-4143-9134-2). Read it in advance of the study to prepare, and encourage your members to read the corresponding chapters each week. In your group, don't let one or two people shoulder the entire responsibility for conversation and participation. Everyone can pitch in and contribute.

CONFIDENTIALITY: In the study, you will be prompted to share thoughts, feelings, and personal experiences. Accept others where they are without judgment. Many of the challenges discussed will be private. These should be kept in strict confidence by the group.

RESPECT: Participants must respect each other's thoughts and opinions, providing a safe place for those insights to be shared without fear of judgment or unsolicited advice (including hints, sermons, instructions, and scriptural Band-Aids®). Take off your fix-it hat and leave it at the door, so you can just listen. If advice is requested, then it's okay to lend your opinion, seasoned with grace and offered with love.

ACCOUNTABILITY: Each week, participants will be challenged in how they love, discipline, and guide their children. Commit to supporting and encouraging each other during the sessions and praying for each other between meetings.

Introduction

Of particular interest to me through the years is a characteristic I call *strength of the will*. While some children have a naturally compliant and joyful nature, others seem to enter the world with what seems to be a tough—even contrary and discontented—spirit.

This distinctive was my inspiration in writing *The Strong-Willed Child* in 1978. And since the book's first release, significant changes in scientific understanding of inborn temperaments have added clarity and new insights. These changes have been included in updated versions of the book. Because it has been so long since that first edition, many strong-willed children are now parenting strong-willed children of their own!

Today's culture is aggressively engaged in an expanding and dangerous battle for the hearts and minds of our children. Now more than ever, many parents are overwhelmed, looking for and needing wisdom and guidance to illumine their parenting path. This Bible study provides a biblical framework for two guiding principles: love and control.

Let's begin with foundational truths that should be the perspective from which we approach all children, including strong-willed ones:

1. Our children are born sinners, full of selfishness and rebellion, just as we are. And we all desperately need a Savior.
2. Jesus is the only Savior. Through His atoning sacrifice, Jesus is the only One who can rescue anyone from sin—including you, me, and our children. Only He can transform a life.

Jesus has commanded us to make disciples, and this discipleship starts in our homes. Christ's desire is that we show and share the love of Christ with our children every day.

Our unmistakable mission as Christian parents is to help our kids see their need for Christ and to teach them what it really means to follow

Him. Any success in this grand purpose requires dependence on the Lord for His perfect guidance.

Parenthood *is* overwhelming. Our dreams of perfection and peace do not play out into everyday reality. Maybe the difficulty and discouragement of parenting has surprised you; perhaps it's just what you expected. Issues related to parenting a strong-willed child intensify these feelings. You are looking for practical answers.

Every day parents ask questions such as:
- How do we become faithful stewards of the children God has entrusted to us?
- What can we do introduce our children to the God who created them and wants a personal relationship with them?
- How do we set a godly example worth following?
- How can we benefit from child development research and other parents who are walking this path?

This Bible study will address these questions and others. Our time together will likely raise some new questions as well as provide direction in your parenting journey.

> "Teach a youth about the way he should go; even
> when he is old he will not depart from it."
> **PROVERBS 22:6**

I pray that the next four weeks will be extremely helpful as you seek to teach your child "about the way he should go." Now let's get started!

WEEK 1

CHILDISH
OR DEFIANT
BEHAVIOR?

● **BEFORE YOU BEGIN,** get acquainted and pray with your group. Ask God to give all parents His wisdom, direction, and encouragement.

Children love to push boundaries. As loving parents, eager for their best and for their safety, we give our children rules to follow. But there are days when our kids push back, rebel, and disobey.

> What boundaries did your parents set for you when you were growing up? How did you push back? How did they react?

Part of growing up is to seek independence by testing boundaries. While some children seem to be born compliant and easy-going, others arrive on the scene defiant and resistant to authority—and don't improve much over time despite weary parents' best efforts. This strong-willed child is the primary focus of our study.

> How would you describe a strong-willed child?

As sinners, we are all born with a *will* that is selfish, desiring to get and go our own way. While its intensity varies, a child makes his will known in the earliest days of life. Willfulness seems built into the nature of some kids. It must be molded and brought under the influence of parental leadership.

The human *spirit* is different, often being much more fragile. The spirit reflects our self-concept, our sense of personal worth. As such, it is vulnerable to rejection, ridicule, and failure.

> How can a child's strong will be a good thing?
> How can it be a problem or even a danger?

While a compliant child is often crushed by confrontation, the strong-willed child seems to relish battles of the will. Challenging as they are to raise, strong-willed children often grow up to be adults of strong character and confident leadership.

WATCH CLIP 1 from the study DVD and answer the following questions:

All children demonstrate childish irresponsibility. Kids will spill things, lose things, break things, forget things, and make messes. Our role as parents is to patiently move our children closer to mature responsibility in ways appropriate for their age. From my experience, a pleasant approach can teach responsibility better than harshness and punishment, even with a strong-willed child.

> We used a game to remind our family to use their napkins. Can you think of a fun approach to communicate your expectations at home?

> How do you think willful defiance differs from childish irresponsibility?

The difference between willful defiance and childish irresponsibility has to do with the intent of a child's heart. A child is willfully defiant when she blatantly defies an authority figure. She may shout "I will not!" or "You can't make me!" and dig in her heels. A parent must respond immediately to such obstinate rebellion.

For parents to shape a child's will while protecting the spirit means setting reasonable and appropriate boundaries in advance and then enforcing those boundaries in love. At the same time, loving parents avoid any implication that a child is unworthy or was born a mistake.

Shaping and protecting also means that parents are assuming their God-given responsibility to lead their children.

● **CONTINUE YOUR GROUP TIME** with this discussion guide.

An interesting paradox of childhood is that boys and girls need—and ultimately want—to be led by their parents but often insist, by their words or actions, that their moms and dads earn the right to lead them. This pattern has existed for a long time and is especially evident in strong-willed children.

● **READ** Genesis 25:22-27 and talk about the different temperaments Jacob and Esau expressed.

Inherent in children is their admiration for strength and courage. Your strong-willed child cares deeply about who is toughest, and will occasionally disobey you for the purpose of testing who is in charge. Jesus' parable of the prodigal son is a classic story of rebellion and redemption. It also highlights a father's love, grace, and forgiveness. Jesus used this story to teach us about both our nature and His.

● **READ** Luke 15:11-16.

> Did the younger son act irresponsibly or defiantly? How do you know? What was the result?

● **READ** Luke 15:17-24.

> What did the young man do once he realized he had acted foolishly? How did his father greet him?

> What does this story tell us about our nature? About God's nature?

> How can you give grace to a compliant but irresponsible child? To a strong-willed child?

As they develop concrete understandings, young children develop a view of God based on the character and behavior of their parents.

> Knowing the influence you hold with your children, how can you model love, grace, and leadership?

Our children have selfish desires, just as we do. They will be disrespectful at times. They sometimes are sneaky, telling lies. We are fallen people living in a fallen world. Thankfully, God's Word gives guidance for those days when children lack emotional, physical, and spiritual maturity; need loving and appropriate discipline; and depend on godly examples.

SPIRITUAL MATURITY

READ 1 Corinthians 13:11.

The apostle Paul reflected on childhood as a time when he pursued "childish things." The fact is, children usually act their age physically, mentally, socially, and spiritually.

> Without surrendering your God-given parental authority, when is it appropriate to let kids be kids? Share a few examples from your background.

As Paul looked back on his life, he recognized how much he had matured in every facet of his life.

> How do you encourage spiritual growth in your children just as you focus on helping them develop other areas of their personality?

LOVING DISCIPLINE

READ Proverbs 22:15.

Why does every child need discipline?

READ Ephesians 6:4 to discover how discipline, administered appropriately, serves as valuable training.

How can you avoid provoking your child to anger?

Be specific about how discipline based in love works better than angry words and reactions.

GODLY EXAMPLES

READ Proverbs 23:26 for a parent's advice to a son.

Why should parents be concerned about their child's heart and eyes?

A child's heart reflects what he or she loves most. What a child sees and is attracted to influences what is important. Our eyes and hearts often lead us in wrong directions so parents need to guard their hearts and teach their children to do so as well.

What character traits do your kids see in you? How can you make sure you are a person worth following?

THIS WEEK'S INSIGHTS

• • •

- God wants parents to assume leadership in the home and be good stewards of the children He has graciously entrusted to them.
- Boys and girls want to be led by their parents but often insist that their parents earn the right to lead them.
- Parents mirror God's love, grace, and acceptance to their children.
- A strong-willed child provides unique parenting challenges— and holds great potential in God's kingdom.

How can you apply Ephesians 6:4 this week? Ask your spouse to help you see how you might better relate to your child as you correct defiance.

WRAP UP

• • •

THIS WEEK submit your children and your parenting to God. While you cannot control the choices your children make as they grow older, you can control your intentional and specific prayer for them. Pray desperately and pray daily. Internalize Proverbs 23:24-25, "The father of a righteous son will rejoice greatly, and one who fathers a wise son will delight in him. Let your father and mother have joy, and let her who gave birth to you rejoice."

Heavenly Father, help me to mirror Your love, grace, respect, and forgiveness with my family. You have graciously given us children for whom You have a special plan. Replace drudgery with joy; criticism with delight and loving direction. Help us to obey and follow You.

READ AND COMPLETE the activities for this section before your next group time. For further insights, read chapters 1-3 in *The New Strong-Willed Child.* Be sure to read Siggie's story!

COLD, HARD STATS

These findings summarize comprehensive research among 35,000 parents of strong-willed children.

- There are nearly three times as many strong-willed kids as those who are compliant. Male strong-willed children outnumber females by about 5 percent.
- Most parents know very early that they have a strong-willed child. One-third can tell at birth. Two-thirds know by the young-ster's first birthday, and 92 percent are certain by age three.
- Based on this research, the temperaments of children tend to reflect those of their parents. Although there are many excep-tions, two strong-willed parents are more likely to produce tough-minded kids and vice versa.
- The compliant child typically enjoys better self-esteem than the strong-willed child and is more likely to be a better student.
- Parents of strong-willed children can expect a battle during the teenage years even if they have raised them properly. Fully 74 percent of strong-willed children rebel significantly at adoles-cence. The weaker the authority of parents when the kids are young, the greater the conflict in later years.
- In young adulthood, more often than not, these once-angry, resistant kids peacefully rejoin the human community.[1]

Which statistic represents an "aha" moment for you?

Which trend most surprises you? Reassures you?

THE PURPOSE OF
PARENTAL DISCIPLINE

God is the only perfect parent. And we, His children, have rebelled and sinned against Him throughout history. Therefore, we can be certain our children will sin.

The objective of biblical parenting is to be faithful stewards of the children God has given us. He has made them in His image, with personalities, gifts, and strengths unique to them. We ask the Lord for moment-by-moment wisdom to be His hands, as He shapes them into mature, responsible, God-fearing adults. When we remember that parenting is a twenty-year process, we can have perspective with each progress and setback, each success and failure.

In the early teen years, the "fruit" of faithful parenting can be harder to see. When your child turns thirteen, you'll be convinced he missed everything you thought you had taught—manners, kindness, and grace. Then as your teen matures in his own relationship with God, and begins to desire to please the Lord, parents can begin to see growth and spiritual maturity.

What a rich experience in life to watch such truths take root, blossom, and grow throughout our children's lives.

> The next time you see new growth in your yard or on a walk in the park, recall this analogy. Acknowledge ways your children are growing and internalizing truth.

CHILDREN NEED LOVE AND CONTROL

When parents exercise strong authoritarian control, children fearfully suffer under complete domination. They become incapable of making their own decisions, and their personality is squelched under the boot heel of unloving parental authority.

But the opposite extreme is also damaging. In the absence of any parental leadership, the child is her own master from earliest babyhood. She thinks the world revolves around her, and she often has utter contempt and disrespect for those around her. This type of parenting creates chaos in the home.

The healthiest approach to child rearing is found in the safety of the middle ground of disciplinary extremes. Children tend to thrive best where love and control are present in balanced proportions. When the scale tips in either direction, problems usually develop at home.

For more on this parenting style, see my book, *The New Dare to Discipline.*

EXAMINE YOUR EXAMPLE

The apostle Paul instructed, "Imitate me, as I also imitate Christ" (1 Cor. 11:1). Start by looking closely at your personal example.

PRAYER
I spend time in personal prayer.

1	2	3	4	5
Infrequently		Several days a week		Every day
1	2	3	4	5

I show and teach my children how to pray.

BIBLE READING AND STUDY
I read and study the Bible.

1	2	3	4	5
Infrequently		Several days a week		Every day
1	2	3	4	5

I teach my kids the importance of reading and studying the Bible.

CHURCH INVOLVEMENT
I serve in my church.

1	2	3	4	5
Infrequently		Several times a year		Faithful in ministry
1	2	3	4	5

I teach my kids the meaning and value of church involvement.

DISCIPLE-MAKING
I lead other people to know and follow Christ.

1	2	3	4	5
Not at all		Sometimes		Consistently
1	2	3	4	5

I teach my kids what it means to "make disciples of all nations."

GIVING

I give generously and sacrificially to God's work locally and globally.

1	2	3	4	5
Not at all		Sporadically		Consistently

1	2	3	4	5

I teach my children how to establish the joy and discipline of generous and sacrificial giving.

LOVING

I am developing a growing love for God and for people.

1	2	3	4	5
Not much		Somewhat		Making intentional effort

1	2	3	4	5

I teach my children to love God and other people.

PERSONAL REFLECTION

• • •

This week read Luke 15:3-32 with a heart that is open to God. Focus on these great reminders:

We all matter to God. We show great concern about something we have lost if that object is valuable to us.

Our children matter to Him. Remembering this truth will enable us to treat our children with the love and dignity they deserve.

We have been lost and found. Because God values us, He was willing to do whatever it took to find us and have a relationship with us. (See Rom. 5:8.) Don't ever get over His amazing grace.

1. Dr. James Dobson, *The New Strong-Willed Child* (Carol Stream, IL: Tyndale House Publishers, Inc.), 49-50.

WEEK 2
WHO'S IN
CHARGE?

● **START YOUR GROUP TIME** by discussing what participants discovered in their Reflect homework.

The spiritual disciplines you examined last week help you grow more like Jesus. Small-group Bible study experiences like this one also will help strengthen your parenting resolve as you study the Bible and learn how God is working in other parents' lives.

> How is parenting different from what you thought it would be? What challenges do you wish you had been better prepared to handle?

> How did your children challenge your authority this week? What did you do?

Your child will feel frustration and anger at times. What should you do? First, calmly listen to his or her viewpoint; those feelings are likely legitimate and a child needs to hear your validation. Any child needs to know how to vent feelings without sacrificing parental respect.

As parents, we must speak truth to our children, reminding them that acting violently or disrespectfully is unacceptable. We can and should be a role model, expressing our own emotions with self-control when we are angry or disheartened. Be big enough to apologize if you are in the wrong in a specific situation.

The need for loving leadership in the home is evident throughout the Bible. (See Col. 3:20; 1 Tim. 3:4-5.) Children who acknowledge godly examples in the home and other settings are more inclined to yield to the benevolent leadership of God Himself.

● **WATCH CLIP 2** from the study DVD and answer the following questions:

What are some healthy ways parents respond when children test their authority? Unhealthy ways?

Even the most compliant child will eventually ask, by words or actions, "What will you do if I don't obey you?" Without question, kids want to find out if their parents really mean what they say.

Jackson talks back, yells, and argues about the silliest things. No matter how many times his mom and dad talk to him, there are moments each day when he uses a disrespectful tone or words.

Jackson loves cookies. Right before supper, he opens the pantry and grabs a cookie. Seeing that he is about to take a bite, Jackson's mom emphatically says, "No, Jackson! Wait until after supper." Jackson does not want to wait, screaming: "No way! I want a cookie now!"

How should Jackson's parents respond? How can they stay consistent as they encourage a respectful spirit and show Jackson they mean what they say?

Parenting experts and studies have not given enough attention, in my opinion, to the root of willful defiance: the sinful nature of children.

● **CONTINUE YOUR GROUP TIME** with this discussion guide.

Sin is the one problem that affects everyone on the planet. All of us, including our children, have a sinful nature. (It doesn't take long to figure that out, does it?) Understanding the sin nature behind willful defiance gives parents a better sense of why strong-willed children behave the way they do.

Genesis 3 recounts the tragic reality of humanity's willful rebellion and the consequences that will forever impact history. God created Adam and Eve so He could have a personal relationship with them. For this couple, life was not just good, it was perfect. God permitted them to eat from any tree in the garden of Eden, with one exception: "the tree of the knowledge of good and evil" (Gen. 2:16-17).

● **READ** Genesis 3:1-7.

What specific words the serpent used to deceive Adam and Eve?

Satan enticed Adam and Eve to sin by countering God's commands and telling them what they wanted to hear ("You will not die" and "You will be like God"). Satan is still a liar today. He says things like:
- "There are many paths to eternal life."
- "You can't believe everything the Bible says."
- "You can be a Christian without serving in the church."
- "There's no need to actually follow Jesus."

What are some lies Satan whispers to you?

How are you equipping your children to know truth so that they are not easily deceived? How do you stay grounded in God's Word?

Look again at Genesis 3:6. Immediately before she took a bite of the fruit, on what was Eve focused?

Eve's eyes were focused on the beauty and delight of the tree. She saw something appealing, something only God possessed—knowledge of good and evil. Her eyes deceived her and her heart turned from God.

We often define sin according to personal preferences or we misunderstand it completely. Sin is disobeying God and taking control of our lives instead. Sin means desiring something or someone more than we want God.

How does our culture view sin? How do you define it?

How do you explain sin to your children (according to their ages)? Why does your child need a biblical understanding of sin?

Our Creator teaches us that we are born in sin, having inherited a disobedient nature from Adam. According to the apostle Paul, we all possess this sinful nature: "For all have sinned and fall short of the glory of God" (Rom. 3:23).

This tendency toward self-will is the essence of original sin that permeates our families. Therefore, our children are naturally inclined toward rebellion, selfishness, dishonesty, aggression, exploitation, and greed. Kids don't have to be taught these behaviors; they are natural expressions of our humanness.

> **How are you making your children aware of the seriousness of sin and its radical impact on every area of their lives?**

I still remember, when I was about nine years old, my mother telling me the story of Samson and his great power and how he fell into sin, repented before God, and was forgiven. While Samson regained his strength, he never regained his sight or freedom. He and his enemies died together under the weight of the temple's massive collapse.

"There are terrible consequences to sin," she told me. "Even if you repent and are forgiven, you will suffer for breaking the laws of God. They are there to protect you.

"If you jump from a ten-story building, you can be certain that you will crash when you hit the ground. It is inevitable. You must know that God's moral laws are just as real as His physical laws."

God is a God of love *and* a God of judgment.

THIS WEEK'S INSIGHTS

• • •

- Plan conversations and use spontaneous moments for teaching children to hate sin and love God.
- Allow children to hear how you still struggle with sin.
- Affirm kids when they do the right thing. When you have to apply discipline, explain why and assure children of your love.

Use Romans 6:23 as your family verse of the week. This verse is an excellent one to teach children. While it emphasizes the eternal consequences of our sin, it also gives us the eternal solution to our sin problem.

WRAP UP

• • •

THIS WEEK pray for your children but especially take your longings and desires for your strong-willed child to Him. Prayer is your way of expressing that you can do nothing without Him, including parent your children. (See John 15:5.)

Try writing your own prayer. Don't be shy about telling God how much you need Him. Be sure to praise Him for all He has done for you and your family.

● **READ AND COMPLETE** the activities for this section before your next group time. For further insights, read chapters 4-5 in *The New Strong-Willed Child.*

STRENGTH OF THE WILL

The distinction between a compliant child and a strong-willed child focuses on strength of will—the inclination of some children to resist authority and determine their own course, as compared with children who are willing to be led. These temperaments do not have to be cultivated or encouraged. They are natural.

In a family of two children, one is likely to be compliant and the other, defiant. With both born to the same parents, this is a mystery. One is a natural sweetheart, and the other goes through life like hot lava. One follows orders, and the other issues them. Each child marches to a different set of drummers.

Some children are strong-willed, yet they express their assertiveness differently. This child rarely challenges the authority of parents or teachers in an openly defiant way, but is willfully rebellious none-theless. Adults think these youngsters are docile, but internally, subversion is brewing. When no one is looking, these children break the rules and push the limits. Sooner or later, usually during adolescence, this child's self-will breaks into the open.

Let's be clear, however: the distinction between compliant and defiant children is not a matter of confidence, willingness to take risks, sparkling personalities, or other desirable characteristics. Rather, the issue is the inclination of the heart of some children to resist authority and determine their own course.

GUARDRAILS AND LIMITS

For years, extended families lived near or with each other. This gave younger parents daily access to essential role models—parents and grandparents—from whom they could learn on a daily basis. Modern families have moved away from this proximity. Without such ready access to wisdom and experience, parents often feel ill equipped, insecure, and frustrated. Living near seasoned parents would help provide encouragement to set loving boundaries for our children.

Most parents hate to be the bad guy to kids they truly love. It is important to recognize that discipline is something we do *for* kids, not *to* them, as we establish loving boundaries for them.

Think about what it would be like to cross a major river on a bridge that had no guardrails. Where would you drive? More than likely, right down the center of the bridge to avoid danger. Guardrails provide protection. You feel more secure with them.

For children, security comes with defined limits. When parents respectfully enforce rules that they clearly define, they create contentment and freedom in their home.

All of our children need to know that they are ultimately accountable to God. Since the tendency of strong-willed children is to test the limits and break the rules, they need this truth of God's complete love and justice to guide their hearts and their behavior. Ultimately, this is a work that the Holy Spirit must do in them.

> How do you show love to your children by providing the security and protection of guardrails and limits?

SIN AND NATURAL GOODNESS

The Bible teaches that we are born in sin, inheriting our disobedient nature from Adam and Eve. Although this perspective is often viewed with disdain by the secular world, we know that God's Word is truth.

How else do we explain the perverse nature of every society on earth? Bloody warfare has been the centerpiece of world history for more than five thousand years. People of every race and creed have tried to rape, plunder, burn, blast, and kill each other. Peace has been but a momentary pause when we have stopped to reload!

Not only have nations warred against each other since the beginning of time, we also find depressing incidences of murder, drug abuse, child molestation, prostitution, adultery, homosexuality, and dishonesty among individuals. How would we account for this pervasive evil in a world of people who are naturally inclined toward good? Have they drifted into these antisocial and immoral behaviors despite their inborn tendencies? If so, surely one society in all the world would have been able to preserve the goodness with which children are born.

Where is it? Does such a place exist? No, although admittedly some societies are more moral than others. Still, none reflect the harmony that might be expected from the natural goodness theorists. Why not? Because their basic premise is wrong.

A VERY REAL ENEMY

According to Barna Group research (date), 4 out of 10 Christians (40 percent) strongly agreed that Satan "is not a living being but is a symbol of evil." An additional 2 out of 10 Christians (19 percent) said they "agree somewhat" with that perspective.[1]

According to Scripture, Satan is a real enemy who wants to destroy our devotion to Jesus (1 Pet. 5:8-9; 2 Cor. 11:14; Matt. 4:1). He wants to devour our marriages. When Christ-honoring parents are totally committed to loving God and leading their children to love Him, Satan will try to bring that family down.

Satan has a plan. Do you likewise have a family plan for resisting Satan's schemes and remaining faithful to God?

SATAN'S PLAN	YOUR FAMILY PLAN
Leads us to sin (See 1 Chron. 21:1.)	How will you and your family flee sin and pursue holiness?
Entices us to chase worldly positions/power (See Matt. 4:1-10.)	How will you and your family serve God with humility?
Distorts God's Word (See Gen. 3:1.)	How will you and your family know what is true and what is false?
Blinds the minds of unbelievers (See 2 Cor. 4:4.)	How will you and your family show and share Christ with people who are not yet followers?
Causes believers to suffer (See 2 Cor. 12:7.)	How will you and your family prepare for suffering and persecution?

WAYS TO PRAY FOR YOUR KIDS

If you really want God to work in your life and family, then let prayer drive every area. Pray that:

- God would protect your children from Satan's deceitful attacks. (See Matt. 6:13.)
- God would open your children's hearts (see Acts 16:14) to embrace the good news of Jesus and surrender their lives to Him. (See Luke 9:23.)
- God would change your children's hearts so they desire to keep His commandments and follow His direction. (See 1 Chron. 29:18-19.)
- Your children love God with their heart, soul, and mind (see Matt. 22:37) and other people as themselves. (See Matt. 22:39.)
- Your children put their hope in God and not be rebellious. (See Ps. 78:5-8.)
- They acknowledge the Lord in all that they do. (See Prov. 3:5-6.)
- God would meet your children's needs and provide daily. (See Matt. 6:11.)
- Your children would grow to be more like Jesus. (See Luke 2:52.)
- Jesus would lead your children to be fishers of men (see Matt. 4:19) and makers of disciples. (See Matt. 28:19-20.)

PERSONAL REFLECTION

• • •

Every night this week, go into the room after your strong-willed child has fallen sleep. Lay your hands on her and pray that the Holy Spirit would conquer her strong will while not destroying her spirit. Thank God for making her the way she is. This week watch for any changes in your child's behavior and in your attitude toward her.

---

1. "Most American Christians Do Not Believe that Satan or the Holy Spirit Exist," *Barna Group* (online), 10 April 2009 [cited 9 June 2014]. Available from the Internet: *www.barna.org*.

WEEK 3

GOOD

· · · · · · · · · · · · · · · ·

NEWS FOR ALL

● **START YOUR GROUP TIME** by discussing what participants discovered in their Reflect homework.

> How is your strong-willed child like you and/or your spouse?

> Discuss a recent outrageous or defiant act your child committed. How did you feel in the heat of the moment? In the aftermath?

When our children are born, we have one major goal: to be a good mom or dad. We pour every effort and every resource into that assignment, only to have our beloved child reject our leadership almost from birth and engage in a never-ending battle of wills. That is terribly painful. It produces great guilt and self-condemnation.

It helps when we confess that, to one degree or another, we are all strong-willed children and that gets us into trouble. Thankfully, God has provided a solution.

WATCH CLIP 3 from the study DVD and answer the following questions:

A strong-willed child has great potential for character development, accomplishments, and leadership. In some regards, he may be better equipped to cope with life than his compliant counterpart.

> **Do you recognize your child's potential? Does he or she know that you do? In what ways are you your child's best cheerleader?**

No matter whether your child is compliant or defiant, your priority remains the same: to use the parental authority God gave you to love your child, help him control impulses, and shape his will toward God.

> **What day-to-day challenges keep you from staying focused on this priority?**

God designed for parents to be the primary shapers of their child's heart and will while the child is still young. As he or she gets older, other people will impact him: coaches, teachers, pastors, friends. Reflect on and record spiritual influencers in your life and why they were important.

STAGE	INFLUENCERS	WAYS THEY INFLUENCED
Preschool		
Elementary		
Teenage		
College		
20s		
30s-40s and above		

CONTINUE YOUR GROUP TIME with this discussion guide.

Parents have a limited amount of time to serve as the primary spiritual influencers in their child's life.

> On a scale of *1 (not at all)* to *10 (extremely well)*, how well are you using this precious season of life to be that influencer?

> 1   2   3   4   5   6   7   8   9   10
> Not at all   Extremely well

Sharing the good news about Jesus Christ is the most significant way a parent can shape a child's will. As discussed previously, parents have a responsibility to teach their children what the Bible says about sin and humanity's sinful nature. But children also need to know the solution to their sin problem. We must share how Jesus Christ can meet their greatest needs: for forgiveness of sin, purpose in life, and eternal life.

FORGIVENESS OF SIN

Mark 2 records the wonderful story of four friends bringing their paralytic friend to Jesus. Full of faith, these friends knew only that Jesus could help this man. They were willing to do whatever was necessary to connect their friend with Jesus.

READ Mark 2:1-12.

> What did these friends have to do to bring their friend to Jesus?

Neither the crowd nor a closed roof kept them from their mission.

> What barriers prohibit Christians today from bringing people to Jesus?

What would you like Jesus to notice about your faith? (See v. 5.)

How can you faithfully bring your children to Jesus?

The key truth from this passage is that Jesus has the authority to forgive sins. (See v. 10.)

What would happen if more parents taught this truth to their children? Integrated it fully into their lives?

How could your children find freedom knowing that Jesus forgives their sins? How can you imitate Christ's forgiveness in your family?

PURPOSE IN LIFE

God created all people in His image. As a result, every person on earth has a purpose. Because of sin and selfishness, many people never fulfill their God-given purpose. At an early age and in various ways, children begin to ask about purpose. We can share Bible passages like Colossians 1:15-19 to answer this question with confidence.

● **READ** Colossians 1:15-19.

What do these verses say about who Jesus is and what He has done for the world?

What does it mean to be created for Christ?

Why is it important for parents to teach their children that purpose in life can only be found in a personal relationship with Him?

How does it reassure you when you struggle to be a "good parent"?

ETERNAL LIFE

The Bible tells us that God has put eternity in our hearts. (See Eccl. 3:11.) God did not put us here for this earth only. We were made to last forever, and we all have two choices: eternal life with God or eternal suffering due to separation from Him.

READ John 3:16-18.

Most likely, verse 16 is very familiar to you. Read it and the verses that follow as if you had never heard them before.

Looking closely at these verses, how would you describe God's love?

Based on what Jesus said, some people will perish (or face eternal punishment) and some will have eternal life based on their belief.

THIS WEEK'S INSIGHTS

• • •

- Children need to know the solution to their sin problem: the good news of Jesus.
- Jesus meets the needs children have for forgiveness, purpose in life, and eternal life.
- The most significant way parents can lead their families is to prepare their children for eternity.

How would you evaluate the most significant thing you are doing as a parent? Are any changes needed?

WRAP UP

• • •

PRAY TOGETHER for God to bring to mind examples of His grace. Recall times you felt unworthy of His love and deserving of His discipline. Consider what these experiences teach you regarding your relationship with your children. Plan intentional time to study God's Word as a family, and pray for spontaneous teachable moments.

Gracious God, we all need forgiveness of sin, purpose in life, and eternal life. Thank You for sending Your Son to meet those needs for me and for my spouse and children.

Lord, turn my eyes away from earthly things to keep them on You. Mold me into the kind of parent who is prepared for eternity and who prepares my children for eternity.

● **READ AND COMPLETE** the activities for this section before your next group time. For further insights, read chapters 6-7 in *The New Strong-Willed Child*.

TEACHABLE MOMENTS

Intentionally look for teachable moments and try to have a conversation with your child about that concept every day if possible. Record these moments, and share outcomes with your group next week.

	ACTIVITY	CONVERSATION
Sunday		
Monday		
Tuesday		
Wednesday		
Thursday		
Friday		
Saturday		

NOSE-TO-NOSE CONFRONTATIONS

In a moment of rebellion, a strong-willed child will consider his parents' wishes and defiantly choose to disobey. Like a military general before a battle, he will calculate the potential risk, marshal his forces, and prepare to attack.

When such a nose-to-nose confrontation occurs between you and your child, it is extremely important that you display confidence and decisiveness. Most of the time you can talk things through and come to a mutual understanding. On the other hand, there is a time to speak in the tone of voice that says firmly: "Please do it now because I said so."

When parents are afraid or unwilling to fulfill their responsibility, the strong-willed child is positively driven to start running things. If you as a mom or dad won't be the boss, I guarantee your tough-as-nails child will step into that role.

Even though a strong-willed child may push you to the limit you must not overreact in anger. Your temper can produce a destructive kind of disrespect in your children. Once cutting words leave your lips, they can be poison that burns into your child's soul for years to come.

> **Read the verses below and beside each one jot down what each says about anger and better ways to act.**
>
> ☐ Isaiah 54:8
> ☐ Psalm 30:5
> ☐ Psalm 86:15
> ☐ Matthew 18:34
> ☐ Proverbs 15:1
> ☐ Proverbs 29:11
> ☐ James 1:19-20

THE PRIMARY RESPONSIBILITY
OF PARENTS

Above all else, we must introduce our kids to Jesus Christ, ground them thoroughly in the principles of faith, and then disciple them in their own faith. This is the most significant calling of all Christian parents, those with strong-willed children as well as those with compliant children.

Our spiritual training should begin before children can even comprehend what it is all about. They should grow up seeing their parents on their knees before God, talking to Him. They will learn quickly and never forget what they have seen and heard. Even if they reject their faith later, the seeds planted during those early years will be with them for the rest of their lives. This is why we are instructed to "bring them up in the training and instruction of the Lord" (Eph. 6:4).

Our children's world should sparkle with references to Jesus and to faith: "These words that I am giving you today are to be in your heart. Repeat them to your children. Talk about them when you sit in your house and when you walk along the road, when you lie down and when you get up. Bind them as a sign on your hand and let them be a symbol on your forehead. Write them on the doorposts of your house and on your gates" (Deut. 6:6-9).

References to spiritual matters are not reserved for Sunday morning or a bedtime prayer. They permeate our conversation and are woven into the fabric of our lives. Our children want to know what is most important to us. If we hope to instill within them a faith that will last a lifetime, then they must see and feel our passion for God.

As a corollary to that principle, children miss nothing in sizing up their parents. If we are only half convinced of our beliefs, they will quickly discern that. Any ethical weak spot—any indecision or lack of integrity on our part—will be magnified in our sons and daughters. Our children will eventually make their own choices in their life, but their decisions are strongly influenced by the foundation we have laid.

LUKE 15 AND SIBLING RIVALRY

A rebellious child usually makes the compliant youngster harder to handle. And even though the compliant child "goes along with the program," he may accumulate a backlog of resentment through the years. Isn't this what happened to the older brother in Luke 15:11-32?

The disciplined elder brother resented the spoiled brat who got everything he asked for; yet, he kept his thoughts to himself. He did not want to upset his father. Then came the day he overhead little brother asking for his entire inheritance in one lump sum. *What audacity*, he must have thought, even more amazed when the request was granted. The elder brother was furious, knowing his little brother's departure would mean extra work for him. *It's not fair that the load should fall on me*, he fumed.

Then the younger brother realized his sin and decided to return in full contrition. But when he was a long way from home, his father saw him, ran to him, embraced him, and placed royal robes on him. The father even killed a fatted calf for a great feast. The compliant brother could take it no more: his brother had gained what he could not—the love and approval of his father. His spirit was wounded.

While the drama of sibling rivalry cannot be cured, it can be "treated."

1. DON'T INFLAME THE NATURAL JEALOUSY OF CHILDREN. Avoid comparing children unfavorably with each other. In matters of beauty, brains, athletic ability, and anything else valued at home and in the neighborhood, children should know that, in their parents' eyes, they are equally loved, respected, and valued.

2. ESTABLISH A WORKABLE SYSTEM OF JUSTICE AT HOME. One of the most important responsibilities of parents is to establish an equitable sense of justice and a balance of power at home. There should be reasonable rules that are enforced fairly for each family member (for example, a child is never allowed to make fun of a sibling in a destructive way; each child's room is his/her own property). Laws in a

society are established to protect people from each other, and a family is a minisociety with the same requirements for property rights and physical protection.

3. RECOGNIZE THAT THE HIDDEN TARGET OF SIBLING RIVALRY IS YOU.
A child who fights with her siblings could actually be begging for a parent's attention. Make a deliberate effort to spend one-on-one time with her: play a game, read a book, paint nails, or go on a nature walk. This special connection creates security and can diffuse the need to fight with siblings.

PERSONAL REFLECTION
• • •

Celebrate the differences in all your children, including your strong-willed child. This week look for ways to affirm them for the potential they hold in the future as well as for the caring, positive actions they show now.

WEEK 4

LET LOVE BE YOUR GUIDE

● **START YOUR GROUP TIME** by discussing what participants discovered in their Reflect homework.

> If someone outside your family were to observe you, would he or she think you have a favorite child? (See Gen. 37:1-11 for a classic case of favoritism.)

> How do you keep from playing the comparison game?

> What will be the hardest part of setting your child free some day? Who will have the harder time—you or your spouse?

Your strong-willed child will be grown and out of your home before you know it. While he is still under your roof, continue to pursue and work on your relationship with him. Don't let him stray too far from you emotionally. Don't ever write him off, even when your every impulse is to do just that. He may need you more now than ever.

● **WATCH CLIP 4** from the study DVD and answer the
following questions:

How do family and friends show their understanding
of your challenges in parenting a strong-willed child?

What do they say or do that gives you hope and
lightens your burden? What do you wish they would
say or do?

These proven steps in parenting a strong-willed child capsule the
concepts we have discussed in greater detail throughout this study.

1. Begin teaching respect for authority while your children are very
   young. Responding to defiance with confidence and decisiveness
   is for your child's good.
2. Define boundaries before enforcing them.
3. Distinguish between willful defiance and childish irresponsibility.
4. Reassure and teach after the confrontation is over.
5. Avoid impossible demands.
6. Let love be your guide!

Based on these principles, how can you show each
child that he or she is precious and loved?

● **CONTINUE YOUR GROUP TIME** with this discussion guide.

God's Word is our perfect help as we seek practical wisdom, patient love, and persevering faith with our children.

PRACTICAL WISDOM

● **READ** Proverbs 9:9-10.

> If you want to gain wisdom, what is the first step?
> What does it look like to fear the Lord?

The *HCSB Study Bible* explains, "The fear of the Lord involves love, awe, reverence, and love of God. It accompanies knowledge, humility, obedience, and blessing" (Prov. 8:13; 10:27; 14:26-27; 16:6; 19:23; 22:4).[1]

● **READ** Proverbs 1:5-7.

Wise parents increase in learning (v. 5) while foolish parents despise instruction (v. 7).

> What are some ways to continue learning as this study draws to a close?

● **READ** Proverbs 2:6-8 and Proverbs 3:5-6.

> If trusting God is the only way to become wise parents, then why are we often tempted to place our trust elsewhere?

The only understanding to lean on for direction is that which comes from the Lord. Anything else can lead to disaster, and certainly to missing God's best for us.

PATIENT LOVE

First Corinthians 13 describes love as selfless and giving under any and all circumstances. God expects parents to train and discipline their children. But it's possible to train and discipline without love.

● **READ** 1 Corinthians 13:1-7.

> Why is it critical that love drive everything a parent does? Why is patience (v. 4) so difficult to maintain?

Loving parents want God's best for their children. Dream for a minute about what you want your children to be like when they are eighteen.

> Does your dream reflect what you want for your children or what God wants?

PERSEVERING FAITH

Christians "walk by faith, not by sight" (2 Cor. 5:7). Hebrews 11, often called the Hall of Faith chapter, is full of examples of men and women who showed consistent faith. Just reading a portion of this chapter will inspire you to be a parent who walks by faith through the peaks and valleys of life.

> Ask the Lord for the gift of deeper faith in Him.

● **READ** Hebrews 11:6-19 to learn more about the lives of Noah, Abraham, and Sarah.

What do we learn about faith from their examples?

Living by faith means living in absolute confidence that God is faithful to give us what we need, even though we do not know the outcome.

How is it possible to have certain faith in God when life is so uncertain?

The opposite of faith is worry. When we worry (and we all do), we are saying to God, "I don't trust You."

What does Jesus say we should do instead of worry?

Jesus gives us the antidote to worry: "So don't worry, saying, 'What will we eat?' or 'What will we drink?' or 'What will we wear?' For the idolaters eagerly seek all these things, and your heavenly Father knows that you need them. But seek first the kingdom of God and His righteousness, and all these things will be provided for you." (Matt. 6:31-33).

Discuss ways you and your family can make seeking the kingdom of God a priority.

THIS WEEK'S INSIGHTS

• • •

- You are preparing your child for the time he will no longer be under your care. Let love be your guide.
- The only understanding to lean on for direction is that which comes from the Lord.
- God is faithful to give you what you need.
- Continue to utilize the six proven principles described on page 47 and in the video segment.

How will you commit to let love continue to guide your parenting?

WRAP UP

• • •

PRAY TOGETHER for wisdom as you seek God's best for all your children. (See Jas. 1:5.)

Heavenly Father, Thank You for all You
have taught me during this study.
Give me the wisdom to apply what I am learning.
You are the only One who can give me the wisdom, love,
and faith that I need to be the parent You want me to be.
You are my strength. You are my help. You are my rock.
I surrender all to You. To You be the glory, Amen.

● **FOR FURTHER INSIGHTS,** read chapters 8-9 in *The New Strong-Willed Child.* Go back to chapter 1 and read Siggie's story again!

This week's video offers an introduction to six principles for shaping the will of a strong-willed child. This content unpacks these guidelines.

1. BEGIN TEACHING RESPECT FOR AUTHORITY WHILE CHILDREN ARE VERY YOUNG. The most urgent advice I can give parents of an assertive, independent child is to establish their positions as strong and loving leaders when their children are preschoolers. A naturally defiant youngster is at high risk for antisocial behavior later in life. Her temperament leads her to oppose anyone who tries to tell her what to do.

Fortunately, this outcome is not inevitable because the complexities of the human personality make it impossible to predict behavior with complete accuracy. So I repeat my most urgent advice to parents: begin shaping the will of the aggressive child very early in life.

How are you doing? How could you improve?

2. DEFINE BOUNDARIES BEFORE THEY ARE ENFORCED. Parents must clearly establish reasonable expectations and boundaries for the child. He or she should know what is and is not acceptable behavior— before being held responsible for it. This prevents children from the sense of injustice for being punished or scolded for violating a vague or unidentified rule.

How are you doing? How could you improve?

3. DISTINGUISH BETWEEN WILLFUL DEFIANCE AND CHILDISH IRRESPONSIBILITY. It is natural for children to forget things, misplace things, and break things. When accidents happen, parents should respond with patience and tolerance. Consider helping kids with cleanup or with handling the loss, if needed. These are not situations requiring discipline.

However, when a child throws a fit, runs the other way, or otherwise refuses to obey, something quite different is occurring. Willful defiance occurs when child knows what the parent wants and digs in her heels to do battle and resist. These behaviors represent a willful, haughty spirit and a determination to disobey.

In reality, a defiant child is asking, Who's in charge here? He is blatantly challenging the authority of the parent. Such defiance continues to grow if parents don't respond immediately and appropriately.

How are you doing? How could you improve?

4. REASSURE AND TEACH AFTER THE CONFRONTATION IS OVER.
After a time of conflict when the parent has demonstrated his right to lead (particularly if the child is in tears), a youngster will want to be loved and reassured. Open your arms and hold him close, reminding him of your love. Let him know again why he was punished and how he can avoid trouble next time. This is a teachable moment.

For the Christian family, it is extremely important to pray with the child at that time, admitting to God that we have all sinned. Divine forgiveness is a marvelous experience, even for a very young child.

How are you doing? How could you improve?

5. AVOID IMPOSSIBLE DEMANDS. Be absolutely certain that your child is capable of delivering what you require. For example, never punish him for doing poorly in school when he is incapable of academic success. These impossible demands put the child in an irresoluble conflict: there is no way out.

How are you doing? How could you improve?

6. LET LOVE BE YOUR GUIDE! A relationship that is characterized by genuine love and affection is likely to be a healthy one.

How are you doing? How could you improve?

PARENTING NOW FOR THE FUTURE

There comes a point when our record as parents will be in the books, our training will be completed, and the moment of release will arrive. If our children go to the wrong school, reject their faith, refuse to work, or squander their resources, then they must be allowed to make those destructive choices. But it will not be our task to pay the bills, offset the consequences, or support their folly. In situations like these, parents fall on their knees and pray for their child.

Open rebellion during the teen years can be treated in a healthy way. This conflict contributes to the process by which an individual changes from a dependent child to a mature adult, taking his place as a coequal with his parents. Without the friction that this creates, the relationship could continue to be an unhealthy mommy-daddy-child triad into adult life.

I want to offer hope to those moms and dads who are demoralized at this stage of the journey. First, you must recognize that strong-willed children are *not* a liability, and you should never let yourself feel victimized or cheated by having borne one of them. Do not compare your child with the "perfect" children of relatives or friends; they will have their share of problems in time.

Admittedly, a tough-minded kid is hard to raise and at times may push you right to the edge. But that wonderful assertiveness and determination will be an asset when your child is grown. These kids often possess a strength of character that will help them succeed in life.

However, the realization of the upside potential of having challenging children in your home depends heavily on a structured early home environment led by loving, fair-minded mothers and fathers—parents who are clearly tougher and wiser than their children. Parents who are reasonably effective in shaping the will without breaking the spirit are going to appreciate the person their child eventually becomes.

WHEN YOU NEED AN EXPERT

Any physical problem that increases the level of activity and reduces self-control is worse when children are already inclined to resist parental authority. ADHD (attention deficit/hyperactivity disorder) is one of the most common neurological disorders in children.

Children with ADHD can be intensely loving and extremely challenging at home. Parents with children who struggle with ADHD should feel free to acknowledge that they may need help.

A child with ADHD child may bully or be physically abusive to his siblings. Many ADHD care providers recommend including siblings in family counseling.

Some behaviors and symptoms medical professionals consider when diagnosing ADD or ADHD include a sense of underachievement, difficulty getting organized, trouble getting started and following up on multiple projects, and chronic procrastination; a search for high stimulation plus a tendency to be easily bored; high levels of creativity, intuition, and intelligence; a tendency to say what comes to mind without considering appropriateness, among others. Do not hesitate to contact a professional for advice or medical assessment when these or other behaviors concern you.

PERSONAL REFLECTION

• • •

Use this page to surrender any feelings of guilt or oppression. Do not blame yourself for the temperament with which your child was born. Rely on the only Source of confidence in parenting. Bathe all your parenting in prayer for God's wisdom and guidance. Remind yourself frequently: *God has given me this challenging child for a purpose. He wants me to mold and shape this youngster and prepare him for a lifetime of service to Him. And I'm up to the task with the Lord's help.*

1."Proverbs 1:7," *HCSB Study Bible* (Nashville: Holman Bible Publishers, 2010), 1031.

Key Insights

WEEK 1

- God wants parents to assume leadership in the home and be good stewards of the children He has graciously entrusted to them.
- Boys and girls want to be led by their parents but often insist that their parents earn the right to lead them.
- Parents mirror God's love, grace, and acceptance to children.
- A strong-willed child provides unique parenting challenges—and holds great potential in God's kingdom.

WEEK 2

- Plan conversations and use spontaneous moments for teaching children to hate sin and to love God.
- Allow children to hear how you still struggle with sin.
- Affirm children when they do the right thing. When discipline is applied, explain why and restate your love and value of them.

WEEK 3

- Children need to know the solution to their sin problem.
- Parents are the most important early influencers of children.
- Sharing the good news about Jesus is the most significant thing parents can do for their children and friends.
- God has put eternity in our hearts, but each person has to choose to have a personal relationship with Jesus Christ and receive eternal life.

WEEK 4

- You are preparing your child now for the time he will no longer be under your care. Let love be your guide.
- Friends and family want to support you in your parenting challenges, but may need help understanding how.
- The only understanding to lean on for direction is that which comes from the Lord.
- God is faithful to give you what you need.
- In addition to relying on God, continue to utilize six proven principles for parenting your strong-willed child.

Leader Notes

It's time for a leadership adventure. Don't worry; you don't have to have all the answers. Your role is to facilitate the group discussion, getting participants back on topic when they stray, encouraging everyone to share honestly and authentically, and guiding those who might dominate the conversation to make sure others are also getting some time to share.

As facilitator, take time to look over this entire study guide, noting the order and requirements of each session. Watch all the videos as well. Take time to read the suggested chapters (noted in the beginning of each Reflect section) from the book *The New Strong-Willed Child* (ISBN 978-1-4143-9134-2). And pray over the material, the prospective participants, and your time together.

You have the option of extending your group's study by showing the films *The Strong-Willed Child* and *Your Legacy*. You can also keep it to four weeks by using just this study guide and DVD. The study is easy to customize for your group's needs.

Go over the How to Use This Study and the Guidelines for Groups sections with participants, making everyone aware of best practices and the steps of each session. Then dive into Week 1.

In establishing a schedule for each group meeting, consider ordering these elements for the hour of time together:

1. Connect—10 minutes
2. Watch—15 minutes
3. Engage—35 minutes

Be sure to allow time during each session to show the video clip. All four clips are approximately eight minutes or less in length. Reflect refers to the home study or activities done between group sessions.

Beginning with session 2, encourage some sharing regarding the previous week's Reflect home study. Usually at least one Connect question allows for this interaction. Sharing about the previous week's activities encourages participants to study on their own and be ready to share with their group during the next session.

As the study comes to a close, consider some ways to keep in touch. There may be some additional studies for which group members would like information. Some may be interested in knowing more about your church.

Occasionally, a group member may have needs that fall outside the realm of a supportive small group. If someone would be better served by the pastoral staff at your church or a professional counselor, please maintain a list of professionals to privately offer to that person, placing his/her road to recovery in the hands of a qualified pastor or counselor.

Use the space below to make notes or to identify specific page numbers and questions you would like to discuss with your small group each week based on their needs and season of life.

Further Resources

Need more guidance? Check out the following for help.

ON PARENTING:
The New Dare to Discipline by Dr. James Dobson
Bringing Up Boys by Dr. James Dobson
Bringing Up Girls by Dr. James Dobson
Dr. Dobson's Handbook of Family Advice by Dr. James Dobson
Night Light for Parents by Dr. James Dobson
Parenting Isn't for Cowards by Dr. James Dobson
Temper Your Child's Tantrums by Dr. James Dobson
Raising Boys and Girls by Sissy Goff, David Thomas, and Melissa Trevathan
Love No Matter What by Brenda Garrison
Intentional Parenting by Sissy Goff, David Thomas, and Melissa Trevathan
Raising Girls by Melissa Trevathan and Sissy Goff
The Back Door to Your Teen's Heart by Melissa Trevathan
5 Love Languages by Gary Chapman
5 Conversations You Must Have with Your Daughter by Vicki Courtney
5 Conversations You Must Have with Your Son by Vicki Courtney
HomeLife magazine
ParentLife magazine
The Parent Adventure by Selma and Rodney Wilson
Experiencing God at Home by Richard Blackaby and Tom Blackaby
Love Dare for Parents by Stephen Kendrick and Alex Kendrick
Authentic Parenting in a Postmodern Culture by Mary E. DeMuth
Grace-Based Parenting by Tim Kimmel

HELPS FOR DISCUSSING FAITH:
Bringing the Gospel Home by Randy Newman
Firsthand by Ryan Shook and Josh Shook
God Distorted by John Bishop
Sticky Faith by Dr. Kara E. Powell and Dr. Chap Clark
Parenting Beyond Your Capacity by Reggie Joiner and Carey Nieuwhof
A Praying Life by Paul Miller
Faith Conversations for Families by Jim Burns

Introducing Your Child to Christ

Your most significant calling and privilege as a parent is to introduce your children to Jesus Christ. A good way to begin this conversation is to tell them about your own faith journey.

Outlined below is a simple gospel presentation you can share with your child. Define any terms they don't understand and make it more conversational, letting the Spirit guide your words and allowing your child to ask questions and contribute along the way.

GOD RULES. The Bible tells us God created everything, and He's in charge of everything. (See Gen. 1:1; Col. 1:16-17; Rev. 4:11.)

WE SINNED. We all choose to disobey God. The Bible calls this sin. Sin separates us from God and deserves God's punishment of death. (See Rom. 3:23; 6:23.)

GOD PROVIDED. God sent Jesus, the perfect solution to our sin problem, to rescue us from the punishment we deserve. It's something we, as sinners, could never earn on our own. Jesus alone saves us. (See John 3:16; Eph. 2:8-9.)

JESUS GIVES. He lived a perfect life, died on the cross for our sins, and rose again. Because Jesus gave up His life for us, we can be welcomed into God's family for eternity. This is the best gift ever! (See Rom. 5:8; 2 Cor. 5:21; Eph. 2:8-9; 1 Pet. 3:18.)

WE RESPOND. Believe in your heart that Jesus alone saves you through what He's already done on the cross. Repent, by turning away from your sin. Tell God and others that your faith is in Jesus. (See John 14:6; Rom. 10:9-10,13.)

If your child is ready to respond, explain what it means for Jesus to be Lord of his or her life. Guide your child to a time in prayer to repent and express his or her belief in Jesus. If your child responds in faith, celebrate! You now have the opportunity to disciple your child to be more like Christ.

BUILD YOUR FAMILY LEGACY.

Dr. James Dobson leads you through his classic messages and new insights for today's families in these eight DVD-based Bible studies. Each Building a Family Legacy Bible study includes four-sessions with personal reflection and discussion guides along with a DVD of Dr. Dobson's teachings, introduced by his son, Ryan. Studies include:

Your Legacy Bible Study
Bringing Up Boys Bible Study
Bringing Up Girls Bible Study
Dare to Discipline Bible Study
The Strong-Willed Child Bible Study
Straight Talk to Men Bible Study
Love for a Lifetime Bible Study
Wanting to Believe Bible Study

Learn more at LifeWay.com/Legacy

r. James Dobson's **BUILDING A FAMILY LEGACY** ampaign includes films, Bible studies, and books designed help families of all ages and stages. Dr. Dobson's isdom, insight, and humor promise to strengthen marriages d help parents meet the remarkable challenges of raising hildren. Most importantly, **BUILDING A FAMILY** EGACY will inspire parents to lead their children to ersonal faith in Jesus Christ.

Learn more at

BUILDINGAFAMILYLEGACY.COM

BUILDING A FAMILY LEGACY BOOKS

From Dr. James Dobson and Tyndale Momentum

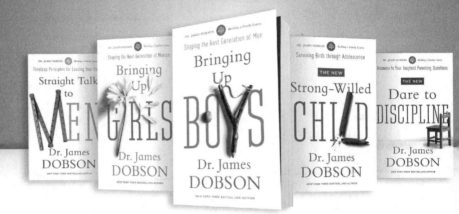

Bringing Up Boys • 978-1-4143-9133-5
Also available in hardcover (978-0-8423-5266-6) and audio CDs
(978-0-8423-2297-3)

Bringing Up Girls • 978-1-4143-9132-8
Also available in hardcover (978-1-4143-0127-3) and audio CDs
read by Dr. James Dobson (978-1-4143-3650-3)

The New Strong-Willed Child • 978-1-4143-9134-2
Also available in hardcover (978-0-8423-3622-2) and audio
CDs (978-0-8423-8799-6), as well as *The New Strong-Willed
Child Workbook* (978-1-4143-0382-6)

The New Dare to Discipline • 978-1-4143-9135-9

Straight Talk to Men • 978-1-4143-9131-1

AVAILABLE IN 2015

Love for a Lifetime
Revised and expanded edition
978-1-4964-0328-5